ISBN-13: 9798683174125
Cover design by: Author
Library of Congress Control Number: 2018675309
Printed in the United States of America

I0491076

To Daralle
My exhausted loving wife of over 55 years
and most honest of ctritics
I never deserved such devotion.

Jeri and Randall
Our kids and my most trusted critics

DONALD LITTLE

Absurdity

Why the GND WON'T Work !

Thoughts and Facts on the Green New Deal

by

Donald Little

ABSURDITY

noun ridiculousness, nonsense, folly, stupidity, foolishness, silliness, idiocy, irrationality, incongruity, meaninglessness, senselessness, illogicality, ludicrousness, unreasonableness, obstreperousness, farcicality, craziness, illogicalness

CONTENTS

INTRODUCTIONS AND GENERAL DISCUSSION

Some of my fellow citizens have the idea that eliminating fossil fuels and byproducts from our daily lives is a remarkably intelligent idea. Being just another of those noted deplorable, stinky Wal-Mart shoppers and, to beat all, a Conservative I have a few points to share with the over-intelligent non-thinkers that purport to have all the answers.

I often wonder from where those 'other' folks get their brilliance. Myself, I spent nearly 50 working years in chemical plants, refineries, and power plants. I have held positions in Retail, Construction, Maintenance, and Manufacturing from entry level to supervision. Some successful others not so. Throughout those years I never forgot what paid the bills...Oil, Gas, and Coal.

So what the hell am I doing here?

Seems as though some rather self-aggrandizing individuals have the idea that eliminating Oil, Gas, and Coal (OGC} will solve any and all problems facing America within the next 10-50 years. All of this in the name of Global Warming. They even go so far as to propose such basic ideas as the elimination of farting cows, horses and other mammals. Does that include flatulent humans also? If so, what's the purpose of the Green New Deal (GND) if there is nobody to enjoy Utopia? What will PETA have to say about the loss of all those furry friends?

My goal here is to point out the weaknesses in the overall plan and just how it will affect humanity. Please keep in mind that I am NOT one of the elite egotistical fools that are making these wild and crazy proposals. Just slightly deplorable and stinky. And by all means I am NOT an expert. Just someone that cares about America using a modicum of common sense. Common sense. Someone once said: "If common sense is so damn common why don't more people have it?" It appears that the GND folks either never had it or if they ever did it was educated out of them.

The GND can be reduced to one question: What will we lose if the entire plan is enacted? Simply answered: thousands of years of human ingenuity and development. Well, I guess that could be overcome. We wait for the inevitable crumbling of things around us and watch as Nature returns it all to the Earth. A move from large and small cities into the abundant caves and cliffs of our distant ancestors. Some of us may even become farmers and grow food to feed some of the other Earthlings. But as you will see later this will prove to be a tough row to hoe. No...not just tough but REALLY TOUGH. Maybe even impossible.

Before we get to the really bad things to result from GND let's consider a rather simple loss.

COWS

Now you may wonder just why this would be of such importance? Maybe the fact that without them there would be NO:

- Leather Shoes
- Leather Clothing
- Designer Handbags and Gloves
- European Shoulder Bags
- Baseballs and Gloves
- Motorcycle Jackets
- Motorcycle and Bicycle Seats
- Seatcovers for the Escalade, Lambo, Rolls Royce   -
- Steak, Hamburger, Prime Rib, Hot Dogs
- Etc., etc., etc.

You get the picture.

No cows equals no hides! Sure we could make some of these items and more from some form of plastic but darn...NO OGC. That equals no plastic. Maybe plant fibers could make a substantial contribution; but, none of that designer crap and worst of all no cowboy boots to scoot around the dance hall floor. Some folks might have figured where this is all going. Most of the GND backers haven't quite snapped into reality yet. They're probably not on the intelligent side of humanity. Maybe they just lack common sense. After all they proposed and back this absurdity. We'll consider more on flatulent mammals later.

So onward into the Abyss.

Say the GND is passed by Congress, signed by the President and slickly crammed down the American Public's throat, what can we expect? So as not to over burden the GND backers I'll take it slow...really slow. Let's look at Coal.

As of 2011 there were 589 Coal Fired Power Plants in the US, producing 1,517,203 Gigawatt Hours or 37.4% of total US electricity production. Numerous laws on the books insure this number will dwindle shifting the burden to other forms of production. This may include Oil, Gas, Wind, Solar, and Wave Generating Plants. Some are really, really reliable sources for electricity. I'm fairly certain that Wind, Solar, and Wave Generation are not in that particular category. More than likely they would fall into the SOMETIMES reliable source.

Approximately 60460 Operations and Maintenance employees are associated with these plants with another 31000 involved in Transportation and 83000 in Mining. That's 174000 workers to be retrained and re-employed elsewhere! Considering an average age of 50 years there are a number of obstacles to employment to overcome, namely possible age discrimination. Also to be considered is time to train and ability to be educated/re-educated in any particular field. Keep in mind that as in the general population some of these folks have limited basic education, high school at best. All of these victims of GND suffer the greatest challenge, members of the largest working sector to be affected; the blue collar worker. All of the GND will surely fulfill the promises of the party of the working man.

Or does it?

CHAPTER 1

Cows and Other Flatulent Mammals

"We set a goal to get to net-zero, rather than zero emissions, in 10 years because we aren't sure that we'll be able to fully get rid of farting cows and airplanes that fast."

Alexandria Ocasio-Cortez

So said Alexandria Ocasio-Cortez. Unfortunately all mammals, because they eat to survive, naturally produce some of the detested METHANE. Some of us, mainly of the male gender, are quite proud of that fact and tend to broadcast boisterously our ability to produce large quantities choosing to share both audio-metrically and nasally offensive evidence of their prowess. In contrast the female gender tends to share silently with little, if any, evidence of the true source, usually resulting in others of the species retreating to a safer non-offensive distance from the suspected guilty party. Lesser (not in a demeaning manner) mammals don't seem to possess this ability or desire to share it anyway. They tend to perform this natural body function as just another part of life.

Cows seem to be the targeted offender among all other mammals. Those big brown eyes are hiding their desire to take over the world and assume the top rung of governance. President Bossie would surely eliminate all forms of humanity considering the abuses suffered by millions of her ancestors. So, one of the main reasons to eliminate or GREATLY reduce cows in all forms is to eliminate their ability to innocently produce ...METHANE. According to the GND this is step one to halt Global Warming, Climate Change, Cyclical Earth Temperature Swing, etc., etc., etc. It'll probably cure Gout, too.

What will humanity lose if there are no cows? Really, if the GND and the elites are as smart as claimed, not much. Just milk, butter, cream, JELLO (primary ingredient Gelatin. Research is required by the reader). Just those nasty old food products. But there are more. Some cows give us their hides, and bones, and innards (the METHANE factory), and beef. No, little Johnny there are no more Hot Dogs, or for that matter Hamburgers. Of course maybe the GND movement may have overlooked the other contributory mammals that could become the new source(s). Oh, bother. Sorry Winnie. They're mammals...and they pass gas. They too have to go. My research turned up this interesting bit of fact that might serve to make my point that we cannot readily survive without cattle or mammals of all sorts.

Readers, keep in mind that the following article was intended for Fourth Graders and should be easily comprehended (big word for understood) by some GND backers.

Thanks to Alycia McClure of Cattle Empire.

The Many Uses of a Cow - Beef By-Products

February 4, 2014

"Recently we had the opportunity to participate in an annual event held in Garden City, KS called farm day, put on an organized by the Finney County Farm Bureau. Throughout the day about 700 Fourth graders from all the surrounding communities come to the fairgrounds to learn more about the agriculture in our area.

There were stations to teach them all about:

- Corn and what we use it for from a local ethanol plant.
- Milk from a dairyman that taught them where milk comes from and what it used for, such as

cheese and butter.
- A large equipment dealer to teach them about tractors and farm equipment and the many different types
- And many more!

All in all, I believe there were about seven different agriculture-related stations.
We were there to discuss by-products and the many ways we use a cow for more than just for beef.

A by-product is something produced in the course of making the main product.

In the beef industry, the main product we produce is beef—the hamburgers, steaks and roast beef we enjoy eating. A beef by-product is something made from a cow besides the beef we eat. To illustrate, an 1150 pound market steer yields approximately 500 pounds of beef. Nearly all of the remaining weight is recovered as by-products.

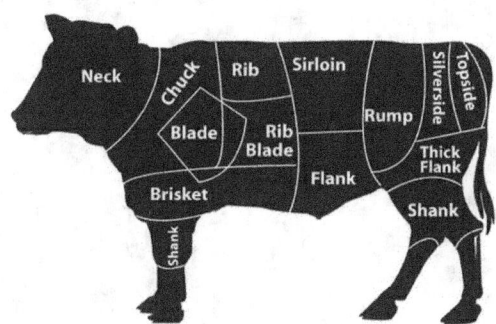

There are three categories of by-products to determine the items made with the rest of the animal: EDIBLE, IN-

EDIBLE and MEDICINAL.

Edible By-Products are things we can eat.

Some edible beef by-products are fairly well known such as variety meats. The nutritious value of liver, kidneys, brains, tripe, sweetbreads, and tongue has been acknowledged for quite a while. Other important edible by-products are less well known. Fats yield oleo stock and oleo oil for margarine and shortening. Oleo stearin is used in making chewing gum and certain candies. Gelatin produced from bones and skins is used in marshmallows, ice cream, canned meats, and gelatin desserts. Intestines may provide natural sausage casings.

Inedible By-Products are things we cannot eat.

You probably use at least one item containing inedible beef by-products every day. For example, you probably know that the beef hide is used to make leather, but did you know that the hide also supplies felt and other textiles? It provides a base for many ointments, binders for plaster and asphalt, and a base for the insulation material used to cool and heat your house. In addition, "camel hair" artists' brushes are not really made from camel hair but from the fine hair found in the ears and tails of beef cattle. Footballs, which used to be called "pigskins," are also generally produced from cattle hide.

Industrial oils and lubricants, tallow for tanning, soaps, lipsticks, face and hand creams, some medicines, and ingredients for explosives are produced from the inedible fats from beef. Fatty acids are used in the production of chemicals, biodegradable detergents, pesticides, and flotation agents. One fatty acid is used to make automobile tires run cooler and, therefore last longer.

Bones, horns, and hooves also supply important by-products. These include buttons, bone china, piano keys, glues, fertilizer, and gelatin for photographic film, paper, wallpaper, sandpaper, combs, toothbrushes, and violin string.

Inedible By-Products

Medicinal By-Products are things used by your doctor.

More than 100 individual drugs performing such important and varied functions as helping to make childbirth safer, settling an upset stomach, preventing blood clots in the circulatory system, controlling anemia, relieving some symptoms of hay fever and asthma, and helping babies digest milk include beef by-products. Insulin is perhaps the best-known pharmaceutical derived from cattle. There are 5 million diabetic people in the United States, and 1.25 million of them require insulin daily. It takes the pancreases from 26 cattle to provide enough insulin to keep one diabetic person alive for a year.

Through genetic engineering techniques and research developments, many of the drugs produced from cattle are now being chemically produced in a laboratory, often less expensively than recovery from animal organs. Most of the material used for surgical sutures is derived from the intestines of meat animals.

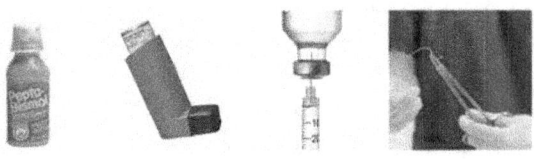

Medicinal By-products

This description of cattle by-products is by no means complete. In fact, new uses are discovered almost daily. But we hope that now when you hear "Where's the beef?" you will think:

• It is in hospitals and drug stores.

• It is helping your car run better and your clothes get cleaner.

• It is in sporting goods, photographic equipment, and art supply shops.

• It is in firecrackers on the Fourth of July.

• It is in your garden keeping down insect infestations.

• It is in soap for washing your face

We really enjoyed spending our day with the area kids teaching them about what we do at Cattle Empire, we hope you were able to learn something as well!"

Well it is obvious that doing away with cows is definitely not in the best interests of the human race. Seems like we would be better off doing away with mankind, womankind, person-kind....political correctness. Life would surely be simpler without the latter...at least until your turn for elimination comes up. Meaningless after, depending on one's belief in the hereafter.

How many Americans are involved in the Beef and Cattle Industry? According to IBISWorld approximately 794,000.

CHAPTER 2

Coal

"We're going to put a lot of coal miners and coal companies out of business"

Hillary Clinton

So said Hillary Clinton in March 2016 at a Democratic town hall in Ohio. Some of you may remember that infamous statement. I'm sure Hillary would rather forget it.

Fortunately this particular statement didn't pass muster for her selection as President. If so Americans would soon learn that there could be a few benefits to keeping some coal, mine owners, and miners around. At least for a number of undetermined years. A closer look into this nasty natural resource may reveal some things that we humans might find useful.

From The World Coal Association:
"Coal has many important uses worldwide. The most significant uses of coal are in electricity generation, steel production, cement manufacturing and as a liquid fuel."

Let's look a little deeper beginning with Electricity Generation. This coal is referred to as Steam Coal. Remember the earlier stated percentage of electricity generated by coal? Don't look! It was 37.4% in 2011. Today that number has been reduced somewhat to about 25-27% due to attrition and in some cases switching to natural gas, an extremely clean form of energy. Having spent about 13 years in a coal burning power plant, I have to agree that coal is not the physically cleanest means of generating electricity. However, it may be the only means of fulfilling some of its other uses.

How about Steel Production? This is known as Coking or Metallurgical Coal. To get a better understanding of just how steel is produced and coals role in the process take a few minutes here to learn. It's on the Internet!

https://www.letstalkaboutcoal.co.nz/coal-globally/.

Okay, you should have been able to read that little tidbit by now and became an expert. Not too detailed for the average reader, but probably somewhat difficult for proponents of the GND. So be it. I hope you noticed the most important comment in the article:

"While an increasing amount of steel is being recycled, there is no technology to make steel at scale without using coal."

Simply stated it CANNOT be done without coal!

Okay, that's two major uses of coal. How about some others, maybe not so large, but maybe just as important products. Things like:

Activated carbon used in filters for water and as purification in kidney dialysis machines.

Carbon fiber. This is an extremely strong but lightweight reinforcement material used in construction, mountain bikes, automobiles and tennis rackets.

Silicon metal used to produce silicones and silanes, which are, in turn, used to make lubricants, water repellents, resins, cosmetics, hair shampoo, and toothpaste.

Other important uses of coal include alumina refineries, paper manufacturers, and the chemical and pharmaceutical industries.

By products of coal such as Refined Coal Tar are used in the manufacture of chemicals such as creosote oil (think railroad cross ties and wooden power poles), naphthalene, phenol, and benzene. Ammonia gas recovered from coke ovens (steel production) is used to manufacture ammonia salts, nitric acid, and various agriculture fertilizers. Other uses include soap, aspirins, solvents, dyes, plastics, nylon, and rayon. All unnecessary for everyday humans. After all we are just stinky Walmart shoppers. However the elites, those prognosticators of 12 year Climate Change doom may find the lack of soap products, cosmetics, hair shampoo, and toothpaste, rather unthinkable and oh so atrociously foul..

CHAPTER 3

Oil and Gas

" We...need to be sure that workers currently employed in fossil fuel industries have higher wages and better jobs available to them to be able to make this transition, and a federal jobs guarantee ensures that no worker is left behind," according to a summary of the plan.

N ow why are these two tied together? My research has determined that they are so intertwined that separating them is beyond my capabilities. Honestly, online research does not provide an adequate division between the two and this product does not demand the detail such research would produce. Therefore put the two together.

So the GND will eliminate using those pesky old, outdated petroleum and natural gas derived products. What could we possibly lose by ridding humanity of such vile products. First of all maybe a few jobs. Not a lot of jobs by some estimates but by others maybe a realistic number in the tens of millions.

That would seem like a lot.

In a study by the American Petroleum Institute the following information would not support the few jobs theory.

"The US oil and gas industry's total employment impact to the national economy in 2015, combining operational and capital investment impacts, amounted to 10.3 million full-time and part-time jobs and accounted for 5.6% of total US employment, according to a study commissioned by the American Petroleum Institute and conducted by PwC LLP.

The jobs total included a 500,000 increase between 2011-15, encompassing both the shale boom and the onset of a downturn in oil and gas prices that began in the summer of 2014. Despite a down year, the industry's total impact on US GDP in 2015 was $1.3 trillion, accounting for 7.6% of the national total.

At the national level, each direct job in the oil and gas industry supported an additional 2.7 jobs elsewhere in the US economy in 2015, the study indicates. Counting direct, indirect, and induced impacts, the industry's total impact on labor income, including proprietors' income, was $714 billion, or 6.7% of national labor income in 2015."

For the mathematically challenged, that equals approximately 27.81 Million unemployed workers under the GND's plan to eliminate petroleum and natural gas use from our daily lives.

SUMMARY

All told only a small portion of the American work force would be affected by the GND. Small being a relative term. America would quickly sink into the Socialist dream Utopia of government domination and prove once and for all that it can only last as long as the other (RICH) man's money lasts. The reality is that ALL 325 Million Americans will be greatly impacted by GND. Oh, and that includes the idiots that concocted this disastrous idea.

Considering the total number of available workers is 132.1 Million. 27.81 Million in Oil and Gas divided by 132.1 Million equals 21%. Hmm. That's getting close to 25%. How would those folks support themselves while waiting for the Federal Socialist Democratic Party to adequately develop training and employment opportunities for just that 25%? But wait... there's more (Unemployed).

Those Americans associated with the cattle and beef industry have to be accounted for to help out the wonderful idea. Not near the massive numbers of Oil and Gas but a meaningful 794,000. Total number of Coal related workers 174,000. Lots of numbers, really big ones and some not so big. Let's make it simple:

Beef and Cattle	794,000
Coal	174,000
Oil and Gas	27,810,000
Total Affected Workers	28,778,000
Total Available Workers	132,100,000

28,778,000 Divided By 132,100,000 Equals .21785 or Approximately 22%

That's 22% of all AMERICAN workers !!

Now THAT is a BIG number. Can you imagine almost one fourth of the American workforce displaced, unemployed, with nowhere to turn except to our friends in the Socialist Democratic Party owned Government? Talk about an experiment in futility! There aren't enough elite professors who know their ass from a hole in the ground to teach that many folks a new profession. There aren't enough class rooms. Well, there might be if we throw out all our students and replace them with the Post GND unemployed.

Let's see, there may be a way this will work. First we have to open a few Fast Food places. You know, where young folks go for a first job. If there is an average of 15 minimum wage employees per fast food establishment and a total of 1.9 Million were open, after firing all the present minimum wage employees, there would be jobs for all 28 Million GND affected workers. Only takes about $16,800,000,000 per year. Hey Rich Folks! Spare a dime? Got that solved. Now what do we do with all those unemployed pre-GND fast food workers? So how soon can we get this wonderful Green New Deal in place so everybody can enjoy all the benefits?

If you have read this complete work, you will have noticed a number of references to the most important product(s) derived from all of these sources. The key word and tricky phrase is *lubricants*. *Lubricants* as in grease, motor oil, bearing grease, slick sticky stuff. Stuff that all moving/rotating equipment requires to continue moving. It is everywhere in everything that has a moving part. Every electric motor uses some type of oil or grease to keep the bearings from seizing. Every wheeled vehicle the same. Conveyor belts that move products of all kinds require some type of lubrication. Farm equipment, lifting devices, draw bridges, home appliances, hair dryers, air conditioners, elevators, escalators, door hinges, locks, automatic doors, automobile and truck doors of all sizes, etc.,etc.,etc. Forever and always. Things will not continue to roll, slip, slide or lift without it. About the only movement I can think of that does not require lubrication is free falling. Hard to collect any work energy there.

So what(?) you may ask. That all means that nothing

in an industrialized country will work for very long. All those electric cars that the GND so lovingly promote needs lubrication for its electric motor(s), transmission, differential(s), axles. steering gear and linkage, doors, locks, power seats. One more thing that just might affect operating that wonderful vehicle...it won't have tires to roll down those dirt roads. Dirt roads that are the result of not having cement, asphalt, or steel. Or bridges. No concrete. No steel. Only handhewn wood. Talk about labor intensive! Oh yeah, how about that wind generator required to generate the electricity required to charge up the Tesla? Needs more of that nasty old grease.

Time for the required sexy part. With all those unemployed folks going to school, there's bound to be a little hanky-panky. What else is there to think about in a mixed gender classroom with a droning instructor telling us the joys of picking cotton by hand, post GND. The results will be more offspring. Why? No latex equals no condoms. No way to transport natural latex from foreign countries. No chemicals from oil and gas to produce synthetic latex (polyisoprene) means no birth control products. No naturally available ingredients. The GND reduced the sources. Ain't no more sheep intestines. Not even those seductive smelling and really good feeling lubricants some of which are derived from Oil and Gas.

I digress.

Back to the dull stuff. If you haven't really grasped the seriousness of the GND, you haven't been paying attention. Once we rid ourselves of all those flatulent mammals, what will the fast food restaurants serve? Remember, we replaced the pre-GND workers with newly retrained post-GND burger flippers. Oh well. Ain't no beef for burgers. Oh boy! More kale! Kale burgers anyone? Are Impossible Whoppers Burger King's answer to the GND? Is BK on the cutting edge of future food sources?

No rotating equipment means no rolling stock. Rolling stock means wheeled vehicles. That means no way to easily harvest or transport farm products to feed the population. Ever picked cotton? Not many alive today have. More folks should give it a try and see if that will be their chosen profession post GND. How about walking behind a mule pulled plow. Forget the mule. They fart. GND will get rid of them. Try plowing either by hand or with your significant other pulling. Gee! Wife. Haw! Husband. How about 100 Acres like this?

Wouldn't this be fun?

Hey! How about fish as a protein source? Brain food! Maybe the GNDers should eat more. Remember those problems with the automobiles? Boats have a lot of the same problems; chief among them no *lubricants* for any kind of propulsion device. No power boats, only sailing ships or row boats in our GND world of the future. Anybody for rowing out to the Outer Banks? Otherwise shore fishing. This seems rather regressive. I thought these GND brains were referred to as Progressives????

How about emergency situations. Think of Hurricane Dorian and the Bahamas. Just how does the GND approach that disaster? No possible way to rescue the victims. No way to readily provide needed supplies, medical equipment. Not anything. Nothing. Zip.

Now for the real kicker. There are thousands upon thousands of reasons to reject the GND. After the flatulent cows and other mammals are eliminated, the oil and gas wells are dynamited, refineries and chemical plants are dismantled, all fossil burning power plants are decommissioned, gasoline and diesel powered vehicles are stopped, farm equipment ceases operation, there is one more item that modern America will miss.

Ever try to harness electricity within a closed space... say an automobile? All that wire used to not only carry power for the motor(s) but also all the little convenience items required to make the driver and passengers truly comfortable requires insulation. Modern insulation is some form of PLASTIC. No insulation means wires have to be separated from each other. That sleek SUV with the electric motor WILL NOT OPERATE without insulation derived from oil and natural gas.

The only means of electricity production will fall on

the only source without moving parts...solar panels. Generators will have ground to a halt without some form of lubrication. That means no wind farms, hydro or nuclear power, wave generation, and especially no fossil fuel generating plants. The ONLY way to make efficient use of the electricity requires insulation, plastic produced from oil or natural gas. So our last form of power generation, the solar panel, also will fall into the GND hole of failure.

Nuclear power plants haven't been mentioned specifically because the environmentalists of the world have essentially outlawed their construction. Not really a problem since without *lubrication* and insulation...they will have stopped too.

Oh! I forgot. Can't build those solar panels either. All the machinery requires that one thing....*lubrication*

Just to really make your day, the electric motors that won't operate without insulation or *lubrication* can't be built. Primary material required for manufacturing is steel. That became a problem when the GND decided that coal was a bad thing.

CONCLUSION

The Green New Deal, when thought about in simplest terms, is a failure before it is even truly defined. Just because some bartender from New York thinks that serving alcohol qualifies her to make recommendations for civilization ending, Progressive absurdity doesn't automatically equate to a good idea. And why do the so-called Democratic candidates for President so easily follow along like lemmings over a cliff? Are they not capable of thinking for themselves? Does Progressive really mean Regressive? Is this doublespeak?

Surely the majority of the American electorate will see GND for what it really is; a power grab. Convince America that in 12 years we will all die and that the only way out is to elect a Socialist Democrat. A Socialist Democrat. Why ruin the name of the Democratic Party? Just call it what it really is. . . the Socialist Party, and present it for what it really is...a means of taking over the American way of life and government and eliminating ALL the freedoms we are Constitutionally guaranteed.

One more thing to think about, if you read closely the article about cows, you may have noticed this statement:

"There are 5 million diabetic people in the United States, and 1.25 million of them require insulin daily. It takes the pancreases from 26 cattle to provide enough insulin to keep one diabetic person alive for a year."

Really sad to see and hard to believe that 1.25 million Americans will be sacrificed annually to the GND when the cows are all gone. All for an absurd and really stupid policy dreamed up by some Socialist idiot(s).

And then there is that **$93 Trillion price tag**. Of course the brains behind this tells us that we can pay for it over a ten year period!

And that's all I'm gonna say on that!

Maybe...

More Information

Cows

www.cattle-empire.net/blog/f/the-many-uses-of-a-cow---beef-by-products&form=IPRV10

www.apnews.com/9791f1f85808409e93a1abc8b98531d5

www.ncba.org/beefindustrystatistics.aspx

www.ibisworld.com/inhttpsdustry-statistics/employment/beef-cattle-production-united-states

Electric Power Requirements

https://www.forbes.com/sites/roger-pielke/2019/09/30/net-zero-carbon-dioxide-emissions-by-2050-requires-a-new-nuclear-power-plant-every-day/#40f40c8235f7

https://www.nakedcapitalism.com/2019/10/understanding-why-the-green-new-deal-wont-really-work.html

More Information (Cont)

Coal

www.sourcewatch.org/index.php/Existing_U.S._
Coal_Plants

www.letstalkaboutcoal.co.nz//coal-globally/

ABOUT THE AUTHOR

Donald Little is a retired Field Service Engineer. He has worked in industrial construction, manufacturing, maintenance, and field service for a major manufacturer specializing in flow measurement and included chemical, refinery, food and beverage, and power production facilities in Texas. His field service involved travel throughout the US and foreign countries. Hobbies include hot rods and cars of all types. He has been married for 55 years and resides in central Texas.